Have you heard their side of the story?

THE DONKEY
AND JESUS

THIS BOOK
BELONGS
TO:

_____

Dewey Decimal Classification: C221.95
Subject Heading: Jesus / donkeys / BIBLE. O.T. STORIES

ISBN: 978-1-4336-8719-8

Printed in China
1 2 3 4 5 6 7 8 — 19 18 17 16 15

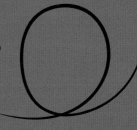

BH
KIDS

EVERY little WORD MATTERS
BHKidsBuzz.com
NASHVILLE, TENNESSEE

Have you heard **their side** of the story?

THE DONKEY
AND JESUS

THE DONKEY
TELLS HIS SIDE
OF THE STORY

TROY SCHMIDT
ILLUSTRATED BY CORY JONES

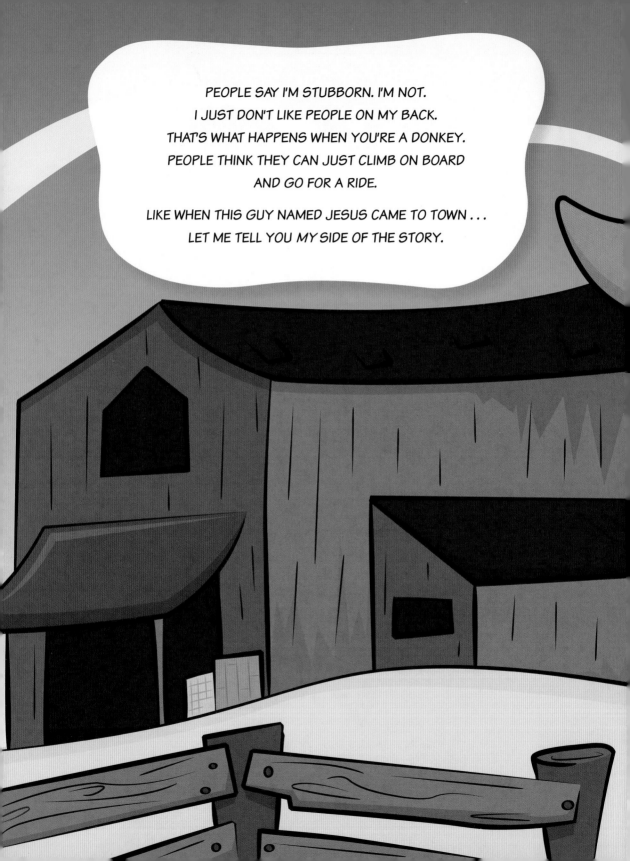

MOM ONCE SAID TO ME, "WHY ARE YOU ACTING THIS WAY? WE HAVE TO CARRY THESE PEOPLE AND THEIR THINGS. IT'S WHAT DONKEYS DO."

"THEN MAYBE I'M IN THE WRONG LINE OF WORK!" I SCREAMED. "I'M GOING ON STRIKE!"

SO FROM THEN ON, ANYTHING THAT TOUCHED MY BACK, I KICKED IT OFF. A MAN, A WOMAN, A CHILD, A BIRD, EVEN A FLY. "DON'T TOUCH ME! I'M ON STRIKE!"

HHHEEEEEEEEEEEEE-HHHHAAAAAAAAAAAAWWWWW!

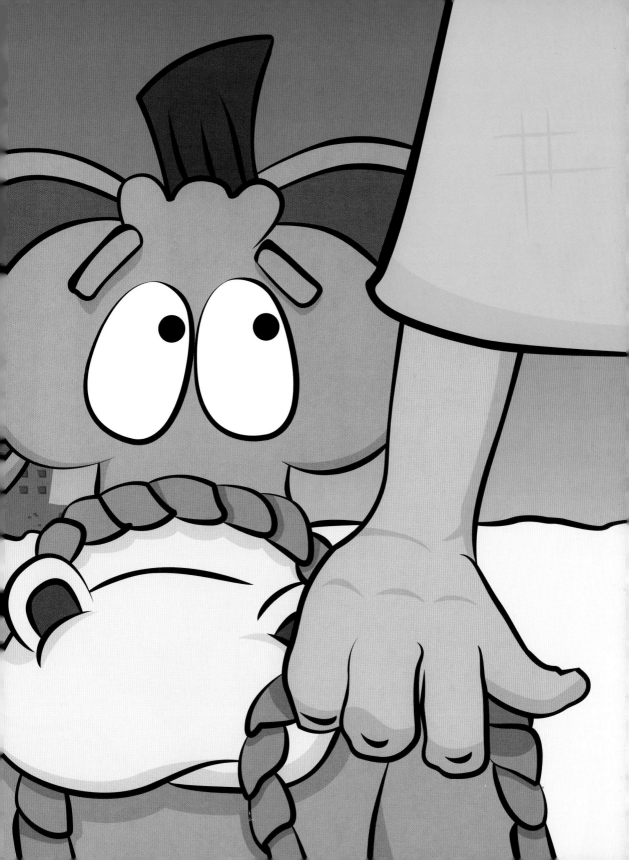

SO I PRAYED, "HEY, GOD, I'M SORRY I'VE BEEN A STUBBORN DONKEY,
BUT I JUST DON'T LIKE ANYONE RIDING ON MY BACK!"

GOD ANSWERED BACK, "I KNOW HOW YOU ARE, BUT I WANT YOU
TO BE MORE HELPFUL. SOMETIMES YOU HAVE TO SACRIFICE TO HELP OTHERS.
CARRYING OTHERS ON YOUR BACK IS WHAT I MADE YOU TO DO."

"I WILL! I WILL!" I CRIED. "I WON'T BE THAT WAY EVER AGAIN.
PLEASE DON'T SEND ME AWAY FOREVER."

"THEN I HAVE A VERY IMPORTANT JOB FOR YOU. I WANT YOU TO CARRY SOMEONE VERY SPECIAL TO ME— MY SON. PEOPLE LONG AGO IN THE SCRIPTURES SAID HE WOULD RIDE INTO TOWN ON A YOUNG DONKEY THAT NOBODY HAD EVER RIDDEN. THAT DONKEY IS YOU."

"THE SCRIPTURES? PEOPLE KNEW ABOUT ME IN THE SCRIPTURES? HOW CAN THAT BE? I'M JUST A STUBBORN DONKEY ON STRIKE."

GOD REPLIED, "YOU'RE STILL VERY IMPORTANT TO ME."

PARENT Connection
B&H KIDS

REMEMBER:
"WHATEVER YOU DO, DO IT ENTHUSIASTICALLY,
AS SOMETHING DONE FOR THE LORD AND NOT FOR MEN."
—COLOSSIANS 3:23

READ:

Matthew 21 tells the whole story of Jesus riding the colt into Jerusalem. Because the donkey was obedient that day, he played a part in one of the greatest events in the Bible. More importantly, he was a part of God's plan to save the world. Imagine what you can do, when you do "whatever you do . . . for the Lord."

THINK:

1. In our story, why did the donkey not like doing his job?
2. Why did the donkey decide to let people ride on his back?
3. What do you not like to do? When are you stubborn?
4. What happens when you choose to be stubborn?
5. What does Colossians 3:23 say about that?

DO:

Chores for the Lord:

1. Get a small poster or sheet of paper and markers or crayons.
2. Starting at the top left corner, in colorful letters, write the words of Colossians 3:23 around the edges. If you have room, write it again until it creates a full border around the paper. (You may want to try it in pencil first.)
3. Within the border, list the chores or tasks that you're supposed to do around the house.
4. Hang the list where you can see it each day, as a reminder that you're working for the Lord.

GOD IS ALWAYS LOOKING FOR OBEDIENT
PEOPLE TO HELP WITH HIS PLAN.
WILL IT BE YOU?